I have
an
idea.

Daddy,
may I
have
the
easel?

Mommy,
may
I have
grandpa's
hat?

Now I'm ready.
I will paint a picture
of God's home.

Some pink...

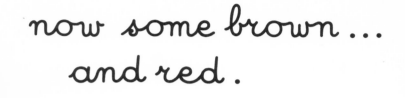

God's not in the sky. He's right here in my picture.

God lives inside
you, mommy...
and me, too!

Mommy

Marty

Daddy

Grandma

Cissie

Tommy

Muffin

Buddy

Carrot